THE STORY OF THE
WASHINGTON WIZARDS

THE NBA: A HISTORY OF HOOPS

THE STORY OF THE
WASHINGTON WIZARDS

JIM WHITING

CREATIVE EDUCATION

Published by Creative Education
P.O. Box 227, Mankato, Minnesota 56002
Creative Education is an imprint of The Creative Company
www.thecreativecompany.us

Design and production by Blue Design
Art direction by Rita Marshall
Printed in the United States of America

Photographs by Corbis (Bettmann, Jason Szenes/epa,
Charles Tasnadi/AP), Getty Images (Bill Baptist/NBAE,
Vernon Biever/NBAE, Nathaniel S. Butler/NBAE, Ned
Dishman/NBAE, Focus on Sport, Jeff Gross, Walter
Iooss Jr./Sports Illustrated, Mitchell Layton/NBAE, Dick
Raphael/NBAE, Murat Taner, Tony Triolo/Sports Illustrated,
Jerry Wachter/NBAE), Newscom (Josh Thompson/Cal
Sport Media, HARRY E. WALKER/MCT)

Library of Congress Cataloging-in-Publication Data
Whiting, Jim.
The story of the Washington Wizards / Jim Whiting.
p. cm. — (The NBA: a history of hoops)
Includes index.
Summary: An informative narration of the Washington
Wizards professional basketball team's history from
its 1961 founding as the Chicago Packers to today,
spotlighting memorable players and events.
ISBN 978-1-60818-451-4
1. Washington Wizards (Basketball team)—History—
Juvenile literature. I. Title.

GV885.52.W37W55 2014
796.323'6409753—dc23   2013039669

CCSS: RI.5.1, 2, 3, 8; RH.6-8.4, 5, 7

First Edition
9 8 7 6 5 4 3 2 1

Cover: Guard John Wall
Page 2: Guard Gilbert Arenas
Pages 4-5: Guard Bradley Beal
Page 6: Forward/center Andray Blatche

TABLE OF CONTENTS

COURTSIDE STORIES

INTRODUCING...

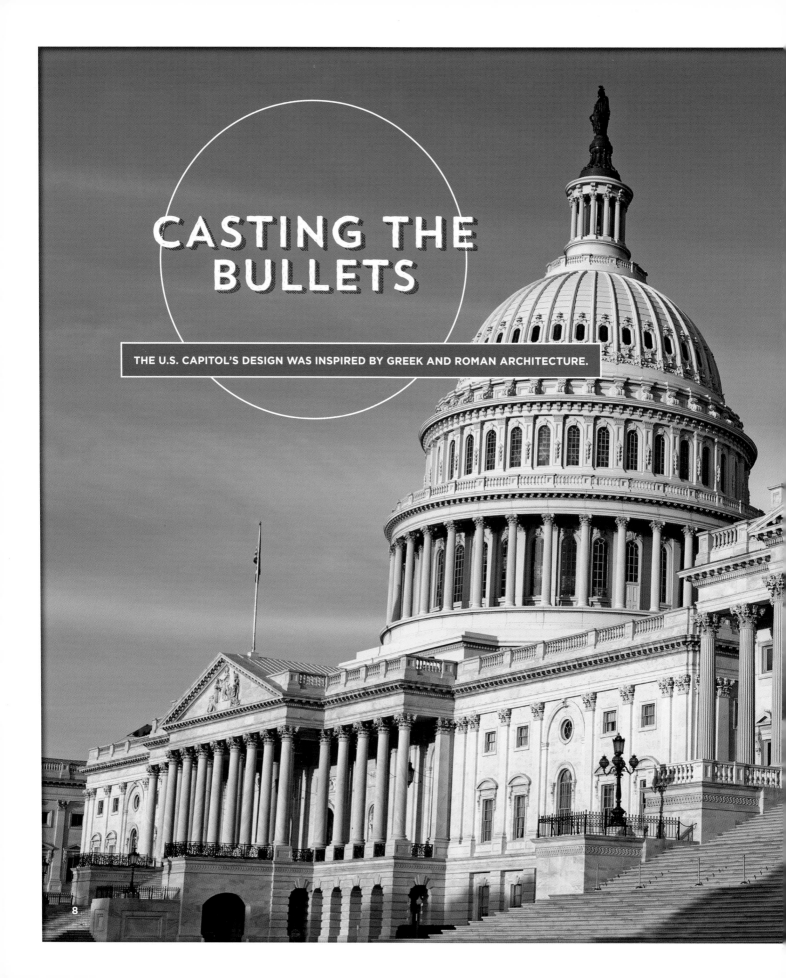

CASTING THE BULLETS

THE U.S. CAPITOL'S DESIGN WAS INSPIRED BY GREEK AND ROMAN ARCHITECTURE.

After winning independence from Great Britain in 1783, the new United States couldn't agree on where the national capital should be located. Southern states wanted it in their territory, but the North refused and demanded that the capital be situated in one of its states. Treasury Secretary Alexander Hamilton worked out a compromise in 1790: The new federal government would assume the Revolutionary War debts of the states, the bulk of which were in the North. In return, Maryland and Virginia would each donate land along the Potomac River to build the capital. This arrangement had considerable opposition from both sides and passed Congress by the narrowest of margins, creating the District of Columbia. The new city within its borders was named Washington to honor the nation's first president. Eventually, Virginia would reclaim

the territory it had originally ceded. While Washington's growth was slow at first, today it is one of the most powerful cities in the world. Many tourists flock there every year to see iconic structures such as the White House, U.S. Capitol, Lincoln and Jefferson Memorials, and many others.

The Washington metropolitan area is also home to teams in all four major professional leagues: baseball's Nationals, hockey's Capitals, football's Redskins, and, since 1973, the National Basketball Association (NBA)'s Wizards. The Wizards were born in Chicago, Illinois, in 1961 as an NBA expansion franchise called the Packers.

The Packers (who changed their name to Zephyrs a year later) took the typical expansion team lumps, going just 18–62. They proved a little more competitive in their second season, going 25–55.

Prompted by sagging fan support, the team moved to Baltimore, Maryland, prior to the 1963–64 season and was renamed yet again. A previous Baltimore NBA team, which folded early in the 1954–55 season, had been nicknamed the Bullets because of its proximity to an ammunition factory, and the new franchise adopted the name. The reborn Bullets struggled for wins in their first two seasons in Baltimore

GUS JOHNSON

COURTSIDE STORIES
BULLETS VERSUS KNICKS

The Baltimore Bullets became a contender when they drafted guard Earl Monroe and center Wes Unseld. Fans were treated to some memorable springtime moments from 1969 to 1974, when the Bullets and New York Knicks met in the playoffs for six consecutive years. The Knicks won five of the six playoff series, but that apparent domination does not tell the whole story. The Bullets forced the Knicks to a Game 7 in the 1970 playoffs, the season New York won its first NBA title. The defending champs then got dethroned by the Bullets in Game 7 the following year. Since the final game was in New York, many fans assumed a Knicks victory. Monroe and Unseld would have none of it, though, leading the Bullets through a nasty, physical contest to a 93–91 win. "It was as good a moment as a player could have," Monroe recalled. "We went into Madison Square Garden, and we beat the NBA champions in the seventh game. It was a close game, but we were the better team."

WALT BELLAMY

POSITION CENTER
HEIGHT 6-FOOT-11
PACKERS / ZEPHYRS /
BULLETS SEASONS
1961–66

Walt Bellamy was the cornerstone of the Chicago Packers/Zephyrs franchise and remained so when it moved to Baltimore. Bellamy was the franchise's top overall draft pick in 1961. The former Indiana University standout was a powerful player, but his surprising finesse and footwork around the basket were his greatest assets. Bellamy charged out of the gates by averaging 31.6 points and 19 rebounds as a rookie. He continued to excel after that, averaging 27.6 points and 16.6 boards during his 5 seasons with the team, and he did it with a smooth and unhurried style. Still, few fans considered "Big Bells" in the same class as great centers of the era such as Wilt Chamberlain, Bill Russell, and Willis Reed. To some, his style could be a little too unhurried. Former Zephyrs/Bullets coach Bobby "Slick" Leonard admired Bellamy's talent but always wanted just a bit more from the star. "Walt wasn't a highly motivated player night in and night out," said Leonard. "He'd have some great games, and then he'd have one where he [mentally] didn't show up. But he was an excellent player."

CHICAGO
FOSTER
PERIOD
3
HOME
3
PENALTIES
LAKERS
CHICAGO
8
25
11
NY

yet showed signs of feistiness. In the final game of the 1963–64 season, Baltimore notched a 108–95 win over the powerhouse Boston Celtics, who would go on to win the NBA championship.

The Bullets featured mediocre guard play during those early years, but their front line was imposing: center Walt "Big Bells" Bellamy and forwards Terry Dischinger and Gus Johnson formed an imposing trio that regularly punished opponents with physical play. Bellamy offered sheer size and a balanced low-post game, while Dischinger was a prime-time scorer.

The 6-foot-6 Johnson, meanwhile, earned a reputation as one of the game's tough guys. "I went up against a lot of the toughest and most competitive forwards and centers in the NBA, and none were tougher than Gus Johnson," said San Francisco Warriors center Nate Thurmond. "I had to go up against Wilt Chamberlain and Bill Russell, so I knew who the toughest players were in the game. Johnson would fight you for every rebound, for every loose ball, and never give an inch. At the time, Johnson was the best all-round forward in the league, bar none. A couple of more inches in height, and he would have been unstoppable."

In 1964, the Bullets traded Dischinger and two other players to the Detroit Pistons for forward Bailey Howell and guard Don Ohl, who always seemed to be at their best during clutch situations. This new talent helped the 1964–65 Bullets go 37–43 and claim a spot in the Western Division playoffs. The scrappy Bullets shocked the St. Louis Hawks, beating them in the first round. They then played tough against the mighty Los Angeles Lakers in the Western Division finals before losing, four games to two.

The Bullets appeared ready to build upon that success the following year, but they sputtered after swapping Bellamy for high-jumping forward Johnny Green and guards Johnny Egan and Jim "Bad News" Barnes. The team bounced back to make the playoffs, but the Hawks gained a measure of postseason revenge by sweeping the Bullets in three games.

INTRODUCING...

EARL MONROE

POSITION GUARD
HEIGHT 6-FOOT-3
BULLETS
SEASONS 1967–72

Known as "The Pearl" for his dazzling play and "Black Magic" for his phenomenal ball-handling, Earl Monroe was one of the most spectacularly entertaining players in NBA history. Monroe was a dominant scorer with the Bullets and won the 1968 NBA Rookie of the Year award when he came out of tiny Winston-Salem State University and averaged 24.3 points and 4.3 assists per game. More than just statistics, though, it was the way The Pearl played that opened eyes around the league. In addition to making the basketball look like a yo-yo when it was in his control, Monroe was able to consistently get good shots down low despite venturing into the neighborhood of towering centers. His secret lay in the uncanny ability to leap high and hang in midair, seemingly in order to buy time and get a better release on his shot. "The thing is, I don't know what I'm going to do with the ball," Monroe once said in explaining his offensive success. "If I don't know, I'm quite sure the guy guarding me doesn't know, either."

THE SPARK AND THE BACKBONE

ELIMINATION GAMES OFTEN PITTED THE BULLETS AGAINST THE NEW YORK KNICKS.

The 1966–67 season was disastrous for Baltimore, which struggled to score and could muster only a 20–61 record. Fortunately, help was coming. In the 1967 NBA Draft, the Bullets used the second overall pick on Earl Monroe, a sensational point guard from Winston-Salem State University. Nicknamed "The Pearl," Monroe wasted no time in becoming a star. As a rookie, he averaged 24.3 points and thrilled Baltimore fans with his array of spin moves, tantalizing high-bouncing dribbling, soaring shots, and slick passes to his teammates. That cast of teammates improved dramatically the following year when the Bullets drafted powerful center Wes Unseld. The Bullets almost instantly morphed from a hustling but struggling team into a dominant one, going 57-25 in 1968-69.

The Knicks swept Baltimore out of the 1969 playoffs, but

Wes Unseld's height of 6-foot-7 was no misprint. He manned the Bullets' center position for 13 years despite giving up several inches virtually every game. But what Unseld lacked in height, he made up for with an overabundance of strength. He was a 245-pound bull who was fearless when defending the lane or going after rebounds. Besides his power, Unseld's calling card was his ability to grab defensive rebounds and fling two-handed, overhead outlet passes downcourt to start Washington fast breaks. The Bullets became a winning team as soon as they drafted Unseld out of the University of Louisville in 1968. The team finished his rookie year 57–25. Unseld averaged 13.8 points and a jaw-dropping 18.2 rebounds to earn Rookie of the Year honors and the Most Valuable Player (MVP) award as well. The remainder of his career produced similar numbers, and in 1996 he was named one of the 50 greatest NBA players of all time. "He was a presence on the court," said Bullets guard Earl Monroe. "He may have been a quiet individual, but he made his presence felt."

Monroe later recalled 1968–69 as the season the Bullets came of age. "The thing that I remember is really turning the corner that year," he said. "When we got Wes, we really got much better. There were games that were very close that we probably would have lost in a previous year, but we started winning those games. I remember how a tip-in by Gus [Johnson] or a tip-in by Wes would win us games. Those guys gave us a tremendous edge on the boards, and it seemed like we got all the important rebounds. I think that gave us the impetus to know that we could win in this league."

If Monroe was Baltimore's spark, Unseld was its backbone. Although Unseld stood only 6-foot-7, his extraordinary strength compensated for his lack of height against the NBA's biggest centers. Once Unseld positioned himself near the hoop, opposing players simply could not move him. The stout center's ability to gather in rebounds and fling passes to Monroe and fellow guards Kevin Loughery and Jack Marin became a staple of the Bullets' game plan, giving Baltimore a fearsome fast-break attack.

In 1969–70, the Bullets went 50–32, and then drew the Knicks again in the playoffs. New York was loaded with talented players that year, including guard Walt Frazier and center Willis Reed. The series played out as an exciting slugfest, but New York ultimately used its home-court advantage to win in seven games.

By the start of the 1970–71 season, the Bullets were a mature and determined team. They went a disappointing 42–40 but increased their efforts in the playoffs, knocking off the Philadelphia 76ers to earn yet another date with the Knicks. The series was another classic, as

the teams again split the first six games. But the determined Bullets went into New York's Madison Square Garden and won Game 7 by a score of 93–91.

With that satisfying victory, the Bullets found themselves in the NBA Finals, facing a tough Milwaukee Bucks team led by two legendary players: center Lew Alcindor (later known as Kareem Abdul-Jabbar) and guard Oscar Robertson. The Bullets had no answers for the towering Alcindor, and the Bucks rolled to a four-game sweep.

Bullets management shocked and outraged many Baltimore fans in 1971 when they traded Monroe to the Knicks in a move that brought swingman Mike Riordan and forward Dave Stallworth to town. While Riordan would become an excellent player for the Bullets, the Knicks seemed to get the better end of the swap. The two teams met in the playoffs each of the next three seasons, and New York beat Baltimore every time.

SINGING A CHAMPIONSHIP TUNE

In the 1977–78 playoffs, Washington coach Dick Motta became connected with one of the most memorable phrases in U.S. sports history when he kept saying, "The opera ain't over 'til the fat lady sings." San Antonio sportswriter Dan Cook had originated the phrase as part of a 1976 newspaper column. It took off in the second round of the playoffs two years later when Cook—who broadcast Spurs games—used it as a rallying cry as San Antonio fell behind in its series against the Bullets. Motta heard the phrase and used it throughout the next two rounds, both to caution against overconfidence during the Philadelphia series and then to keep fans' spirits up as Seattle took successive 1–0, 2–1, and 3–2 series leads in the Finals. His faith paid off as the Bullets forced Game 7 after a 35-point blowout win in the sixth game. Wes Unseld's two free throws with seconds remaining assured a 105–99 Bullets victory. It was the city's first pro title in any sport since the Redskins had won the National Football League championship way back in 1942.

21

WINNING IN WASHINGTON

K. C. JONES'S LAID-BACK COACHING STYLE EARNED HIM A PLACE IN THE HALL OF FAME.

Unhappy with the arena situation in Baltimore, the team moved to Washington, D.C., prior to the 1973–74 season and became the Capital (then Washington) Bullets. They hired new coach K. C. Jones, a former Celtics star known for his calm leadership. Jones inherited a still-powerful lineup. Unseld played a key role, and forward Elvin Hayes had become the team's go-to scorer. Phil Chenier was a smooth backcourt leader, while Riordan scored clutch baskets. This lineup propelled Washington to a 60–22 record in 1974–75 and the championship of the Eastern Conference's newly created Central Division.

After fighting past the Buffalo Braves and the Celtics in the playoffs, the Bullets returned to the grand stage of the NBA Finals. Washington was a significant favorite against the upstart Golden State Warriors, who featured

JEFF RULAND

COURTSIDE STORIES

WASHINGTON'S GIANTS

The 1985–86 Washington Bullets were not the best team of all time, but they were one of the biggest. Few NBA teams have ever sent a taller front line onto the court than the Bullets did when they put 6-foot-9 Cliff Robinson, 6-foot-10 Jeff Ruland, and 7-foot-7 Manute Bol in the lineup at the same time. Great height did not translate into great success, though, as Washington finished the season 39–43 and fell to Philadelphia in the first round of the playoffs. Surprisingly, despite their length, the Bullets did not even win the battle of the boards that season, as they were out-rebounded by more than 350 boards over the course of the season. Robinson, who had a reputation as a journeyman player, enjoyed a great season, averaging 18.7 points and 8.7 rebounds per game. Ruland was even better, pulling his weight with averages of 19 points and 10.7 boards per game. The weak rebounding link was the poor-jumping Bol, who snared only six rebounds per game—a figure that actually represented his career best.

forward Rick Barry but few other stars. In an incredible upset, the Warriors won four closely contested games and swept the series. "It was very hard to take, considering how hard we had worked to get to the Finals," Hayes said. "I'm not taking anything away from the Warriors, because they were a very good team and very competitive. But there was nobody in our locker room who wouldn't have wanted another shot at them. Let's face it: we thought we were better than they were."

he Bullets' run of playoff heartbreak finally came to an end in 1978. The team was starting to show its age, but behind Hayes and forwards Bob Dandridge and Kevin Grevey, Washington still could put huge numbers on the scoreboard. The team played well enough in the 1977–78 regular season, going 44–38, but few fans or sportswriters thought the Bullets had a championship run in them. However, Dick Motta—who had replaced Jones as head coach the year before—ratcheted up the intensity as the playoffs began, demanding that players put a full effort on the floor.

The Bullets beat the Hawks, San Antonio Spurs, and 76ers in the Eastern Conference playoffs, leaving just the Seattle SuperSonics between them and their first NBA championship. The SuperSonics grabbed a three-games-to-two lead in the Finals. But Hayes, Unseld, and the rest of the Bullets would not be denied this time, crushing Seattle by 35 points in Game 6 and managing a 105–99 win on the road in Game 7. Washington finally had its title. "This is why we hung together and worked so hard," said a joyous Hayes. "It was all worth it. From the pain of losing to Golden State to winning the title. That's why you play the game, and it was even better than you thought it would be."

Washington marched right back to the NBA Finals the next year, again meeting Seattle after amassing the league's best record at 54–28. This time, though, fate favored the SuperSonics, who triumphed in five games. Bullets fans didn't know it yet, but that was to be the team's last hurrah. As a new decade began, Washington slid into a long run of mediocrity.

COURTSIDE STORIES

A KING-SIZED COMEBACK

When the Bullets signed free-agent forward Bernard King prior to the 1987–88 season, the move prompted quite a few raised eyebrows around the NBA. King had been a star with the Knicks, but he had suffered a gruesome knee injury that caused him to miss the entire 1985–86 season. When he played only a handful of games the following year, the Knicks felt they had no other choice but to cut him. The Bullets, who were struggling offensively at the time, decided they had nothing to lose by giving him a chance. King came through in a big way. He averaged 17.2 points with the Bullets in his first season. He was even better in each of the next 3 seasons, reaching his peak in 1990–91 when he capped his amazing story by averaging 28.4 points (scoring 52 points against the Denver Nuggets in 1 game) and playing in the All-Star Game for the final time in his career. "To come back after the entire knee was reconstructed," King said, "is something that I'm awfully proud of."

ELVIN HAYES

POSITION FORWARD
HEIGHT 6-FOOT-9
BULLETS SEASONS 1972–81

Elvin Hayes was as enigmatic as he was talented. The explosive forward proved to be the ideal complement to center Wes Unseld in the frontcourt, but he had developed a reputation as a testy and hard-to-coach player prior to being traded to Baltimore in 1972. "The Big E" had not gotten along with the coaching staff as a member of the San Diego (and later, Houston) Rockets, and many people thought Baltimore coach Gene Shue would not be able to handle his volatile personality. But Hayes committed himself to basketball excellence while with the Bullets and proved to be a dynamic all-around threat. He averaged 21.3 points and 12.7 rebounds during his 9 seasons with the Bullets and was even more dangerous in the playoffs. He was the single most dominant player during the Bullets' run to the 1978 NBA championship, and winning the title was the most satisfying moment of Hayes's career. "Finally winning the championship completes the picture," he said. "Because no one can ever again say that E's not a champion." He joined Unseld on the NBA's 50th Anniversary All-Time Team in 1996.

BRUISE BROTHERS, BOL, AND BOGUES

RICK MAHORN WAS A RELENTLESS ON-COURT PRESENCE AND THRIVED ON CONTACT PLAYS.

The Bullets' lineup was reconfigured in the early 1980s as veterans such as Hayes and Unseld were traded away or retired. Two new arrivals ensured that, even if Washington's talent level dropped, its reputation for physical play would remain intact. Center/forwards Jeff Ruland and Rick Mahorn were a pair of hardworking widebodies who often seemed to want to prove their toughness nearly as much as they wanted to win games. Ruland showed a fine scoring touch as he averaged 18.7 points per game from 1981–82 through 1985–86. Mahorn, meanwhile, averaged 8.8 boards per game from 1981–82 through 1984–85.

While Washington fans loved their so-called "Bruise Brothers," many opponents saw them as thugs. Hall of Fame Celtics announcer Johnny Most dubbed them "McFilthy and McNasty," labeling them the dirtiest players

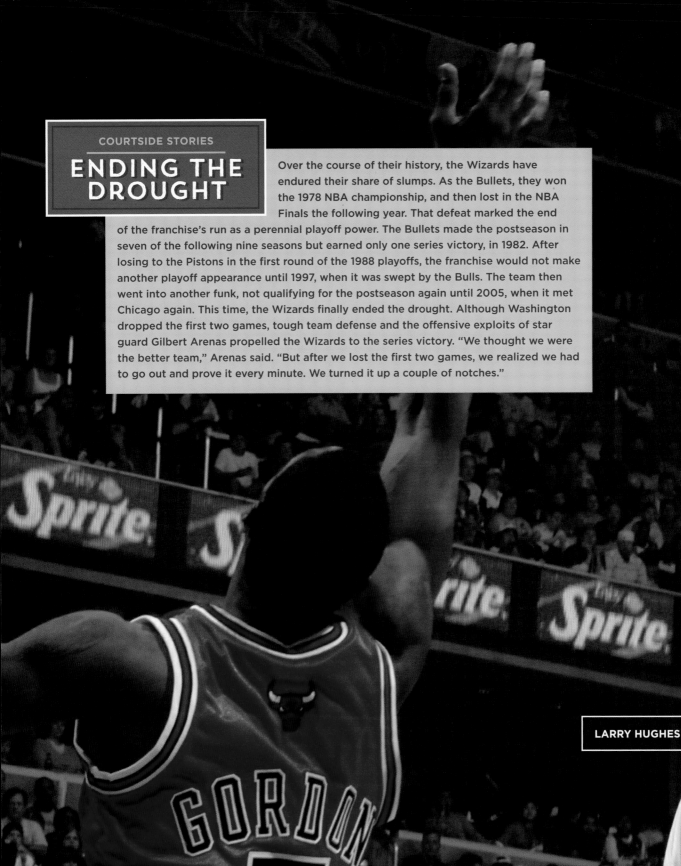

ENDING THE DROUGHT

Over the course of their history, the Wizards have endured their share of slumps. As the Bullets, they won the 1978 NBA championship, and then lost in the NBA Finals the following year. That defeat marked the end of the franchise's run as a perennial playoff power. The Bullets made the postseason in seven of the following nine seasons but earned only one series victory, in 1982. After losing to the Pistons in the first round of the 1988 playoffs, the franchise would not make another playoff appearance until 1997, when it was swept by the Bulls. The team then went into another funk, not qualifying for the postseason again until 2005, when it met Chicago again. This time, the Wizards finally ended the drought. Although Washington dropped the first two games, tough team defense and the offensive exploits of star guard Gilbert Arenas propelled the Wizards to the series victory. "We thought we were the better team," Arenas said. "But after we lost the first two games, we realized we had to go out and prove it every minute. We turned it up a couple of notches."

LARRY HUGHES

MANUTE BOL AND MUGGSY BOGUES COMBINED FOR 569 POINTS IN THEIR SINGLE SEASON TOGETHER.

he had ever seen. The Bullets' frontcourt duo ignored the criticisms, though, leading Washington to respectable 42–40 and 35–47 records in 1982–83 and 1983–84. "There were a lot of people out there that didn't like us, but Jeff and I didn't care," Mahorn later said. "We went out onto the court, and we played hard because we were going to do anything we could to win. We were not dirty, and we did not try to injure anyone. But we were trying to win, and we have nothing to apologize for about the way we played."

A few seasons later, the Bullets featured one of the most interesting teammate combinations in NBA history. In 1987–88, they put 7-foot-7 center Manute Bol on the court at the same time as 5-foot-3 point guard Tyrone "Muggsy" Bogues. Bol was a rail-thin, shot-blocking specialist from Sudan who developed an awkward-looking but accurate three-point shot, while the pint-sized Bogues used his speed and quickness to energize Washington's offense and create scoring opportunities for such talented teammates as guard Jeff Malone, center Moses Malone, and forward Bernard King. The crowds adopted both Bol and Bogues as fan favorites, and they cheered even louder as the Bullets went 38–44 in 1987–88 and made the playoffs.

PLAYERS ATTEMPTING TO
GET PAST THE IMPOSING BOL
OFTEN TRIED HOOK SHOTS.

After falling to the Pistons in the 1988 playoffs, the Bullets would not make the postseason again for nearly a decade. Still, Washington was not devoid of talent. Former star Wes Unseld had been hired as head coach in 1987, and he looked to Jeff Malone and King for steady scoring.

Malone was a brilliant shooter with a quick release, while King was a former scorer extraordinaire with the Knicks who had worked his way back to star status in Washington after a devastating knee injury. "It was just a magnificent comeback," said Hubie Brown, who coached King in New York. "It seemed like he would not be able to come back from the injury, but he did it because he never accepted that he wouldn't be able to play anymore, and he did all the hard work he needed to do."

Still, the Bullets struggled for wins. Their defense was often porous, they struggled away from home, and they seemed to lack the "killer instinct" to close out games. Unseld coached the team through 1994 and was then replaced by Jim Lynam. Washington finally earned a playoff berth again in 1997 with an improved 44–38 record. By then, the Bullets featured a new lineup that included 7-foot-7 center Gheorghe Muresan, brawny forwards Chris Webber and Juwan Howard, and deft-passing guard Rod Strickland. Facing Michael Jordan and the high-powered Chicago Bulls in the postseason, though, the Bullets were quickly swept aside.

CHRIS WEBBER'S SMOOTH OPERATIONS AROUND THE HOOP EARNED HIM A SPOT ON THE 1997 ALL-STAR TEAM.

INTRODUCING...

JEFF MALONE

POSITION GUARD
HEIGHT 6-FOOT-4
BULLETS SEASONS
1983–90

Jeff Malone was one of the most unheralded of the NBA's great scorers. After being drafted by the Bullets in 1983 out of Mississippi State University, he quietly proved to be an outstanding shooter who could fill up the nets. Malone had a signature moment in his rookie season. In a game against the Detroit Pistons, he heaved a last-second three-point shot toward the basket as he fell backwards along the baseline and flew out of bounds. The ball sailed over the top of the backboard and swished in for the game-winner. (Years later, fan voting on NBA.com would name that shot one of the 10 best in NBA history.) Malone averaged better than 20 points per game during 5 of his 7 seasons with the Bullets and was a sensational free-throw shooter, connecting on 86.9 percent of his shots from the "charity stripe." "I didn't have to have the ball in the last two minutes [of games]," the confident Malone later said. "But if I did, I was going to make the best of it."

WELCOMING THE WIZARDS

THE WIZARDS LOOKED TO REBUILD WITH YOUNG TALENT SUCH AS GUARD GILBERT ARENAS.

In the early 1990s, owner Abe Pollin was becoming frustrated with the association of his team's nickname and gun violence. After Pollin's friend, Israeli prime minister Yitzhak Rabin, was assassinated, Pollin announced his plans to rename the team. "Wizards" emerged victorious from a name-the-team contest, as it "portrayed a non-violent image," according to the team's official website. "The name depicts energy and an omnipresent power, and brings to light what is hoped to be the wise and magical nature of the team." The local chapter of the National Association for the Advancement of Colored People (NAACP) pointed out another, less appealing connection: The supreme leader of the racist organization the Ku Klux Klan (KKK) is known as the Imperial Wizard.

The name change did nothing to improve the team's fortunes, though, as the Wizards went 42–40 in 1997–98

MADISON SQUARE GARDEN

WHILE IN A WIZARDS JERSEY, GUARD MICHAEL JORDAN RETAINED HIS FAVORITE NUMBER (23).

but missed the playoffs. Unfortunately, that was the beginning of a disappointing trend, as Washington became a conference doormat in the seasons that followed, despite the efforts of sharpshooting guard Mitch Richmond.

In 2000, the Wizards made headlines by hiring the newly retired Michael Jordan in the team's front office. Then, in 2001, they lured him out of retirement and back onto the court for the first of two comeback seasons. Jordan averaged at least 20 points a game in each of those seasons and teamed with young guard Richard Hamilton in 2001-02 to give the Wizards solid scoring punch, but it was not enough to make Washington a contender. Jordan took his last competitive shot in 2003 before retiring from the hardwood for good.

The 2004–05 season marked the start of a new era in Washington. The Wizards emerged as one of the most improved teams in the league behind three rising stars—guard Gilbert Arenas, forward Antawn Jamison, and swingman Larry Hughes. The trio averaged a combined 67.1 points per game and displayed an offensive versatility that made Washington one of the most difficult teams in the NBA to defend. Arenas keyed the attack with his

confident outside shooting and creativity, Jamison flexed his muscle as an inside scoring force, and the lanky Hughes aggravated opposing defenses with his speed and ability to play multiple positions. The Bullets rolled to a 45-37 record and beat the Bulls in six games, winning their first best-of-seven playoff series since 1979.

Even though the Bullets lost to the Miami Heat in the second round of the playoffs, the team's new youth movement had many Washington fans—and players—thinking big. "We have the kind of team that can win a lot of games together," said Arenas. "We all like each other, and we all want to play for each other. When we played the Bulls in the playoffs, none of us had any sense of panic because we lost the first two games.... We figured if we could play our regular game once we got home, that was all we needed to do. That's just how it worked out for us."

Unfortunately, Hughes left town in 2005, and Arenas was plagued by injuries. Although the Wizards made the playoffs in 2006, 2007, and 2008, they could never get past the first round.

INTRODUCING...

ANTAWN JAMISON

POSITION FORWARD
HEIGHT 6-FOOT-8
WIZARDS SEASONS
2004–10

Antawn Jamison won the National College Player of the Year award in 1998 while playing for the powerhouse University of North Carolina. During his first 5 NBA seasons (with the Golden State Warriors), he twice scored 51 points in a game. When he was traded to the Wizards in 2004, he maintained his consistently high level of play. In that first season, he was named an All-Star for the first time, and the team's 45–37 mark was the best in 26 years. In 10 of 11 seasons from 1999–2000 to 2009–10, he never averaged fewer than 18.7 points and 6.8 boards. Yet Jamison was somewhat overlooked as a star in Washington, probably because he lacked the outgoing personality of such teammates as Gilbert Arenas. Few players in the game, though, were as universally liked and respected. "You're not going to meet a nicer guy than him," said Garry St. Jean, who coached Jamison when he was with the Warriors. "If you told me, in my 26 years [in the NBA], to pick my 5 best 'people' players, he'd be one of them."

SIX-FOOT-10 CENTER EMEKA OKAFOR INJECTED ENERGY INTO THE WIZARDS' DEFENSE.

COURTSIDE STORIES
A HISTORY OF NAMES

The Washington Wizards were born in Chicago as an expansion team called the Packers (in reference to the city's meat-packing industry) in 1961. A year later, new ownership changed the team's name to the Zephyrs (a reference to a Greek wind god—befitting the "Windy City" nickname of Chicago). Chicago basketball fans would eventually go wild for the Bulls, but they did not take to the Packers/ Zephyrs. The club therefore moved to Baltimore in 1963, changing its name to the Bullets (after another NBA team that had played there in the 1940s and '50s). The Bullets moved to Washington, D.C., in 1973, changing their name to the Capital Bullets. The next season, the team's name changed once again, to the Washington Bullets. By the 1990s, team owner Abe Pollin had grown uncomfortable with the violent connotation of the name "Bullets." In 1997, as the club opened its new home, the MCI Center, he announced that the team would henceforth be known as the Wizards, a name that had been chosen above other possibilities such as the Monuments, Express, and Seadogs.

Washington found a new nemesis in forward LeBron James, whose Cleveland Cavaliers knocked the Wizards from the postseason three years in a row.

he 2008–09 season was a dark one, as Arenas missed virtually the entire season with a knee injury. The Wizards limped to a 19–63 record, their worst since 1961–62. The next year was not much better. First, longtime team owner Abe Pollin died early in the season. Then Arenas was suspended for bringing guns into the locker room. Jamison and two other players were traded, and the best player received in return, swingman Josh Howard, promptly suffered a knee injury. Not surprisingly, the Wizards went 26–56. "Next year's going to be better," Pollin's widow, Irene, told fans after the season. "I can promise you that."

Unfortunately, the team couldn't fulfill her promise. Washington won the 2010 draft lottery and used the top overall pick to select University of Kentucky All-American guard John Wall. They also acquired three-point specialist Kirk Hinrich. Yet the Wizards could muster only a 23–59 record in 2010-11.

The following year, they had a 20–46 lockout-shortened record, the second-worst in the NBA. In response, the front office was busy in the off-season, drafting University of Florida guard Bradley Beal and trading for veteran big men Emeka Okafor and Trevor Ariza. Many observers felt that those moves would improve the team's overall defense and add scoring punch. Washington also retained Randy Wittman, who had taken over as head coach after a 2–15 start to the 2011–12 season, because

he was credited with making the team's offensive game more competitive.

The team improved slightly in 2012-13. But the Wizards were still far from playoff contention. One of the problems was an inability to win on the road. The team compiled a 22–19 home mark but won just seven games in other arenas. Another was the loss of Wall to injury at the start of the season. The Wizards went 5–28 without him and a vastly improved 24–25 when he returned to action.

Just before the start of the 2013–14 season, Okafor was traded to the Suns for four players, including 6-foot-11 center Marcin Gortat, who meshed well with Wall, Beal, and Ariza. The Wizards continued their steady improvement, thrilling the hometown fans with a trip to the playoffs for the first time since 2007-08. Even though they were defeated by the Indiana Pacers in the second round, the Wizards were encouraged to keep pressing forward. "When you see it change, when you see the things that you've implemented begin to work, you want to continue on," said Wittman.

After one of the most dismal stretches in NBA history—the team went a combined 117–277 from 2008 to 2013, a winning mark of just 29.6 percent—hopes along the Potomac are starting to climb. With healthy players and a renewed taste of success, Wizards fans are optimistic that the team could reverse its recent struggles and regain some of the stature of the great teams of the past.

QUICK-FOOTED JOHN WALL USED SURPRISING SPEED TO BEAT OPPONENTS TO THE BASKET.

INDEX